A
STRAIGHTFOWARD
TO
EFFECTIVE
NEGOTIATING

A
STRAIGHTFOWARD
GUIDE
TO
EFFECTIVE NEGOTIATING

DAVID BLANCHARD

Straightfoward Guides

© Straightforward Publishing 2015

ISBN
978-1-84716-517-6

Printed by 4Edge Ltd www.4edge.co.uk

Cover Design by Bookworks Derby

A STRAIGHTFWARD GUIDE TO EFFECTIVE NEGOTIATING

CONTENTS

Foreword
The Stepping Stones to Successful Negotiation

1. EFFECTIVE NEGOTIATION TECHNIQUES

A Summary of Effective Negotiating Techniques   **19**

Preparation is key   19

Have a strategy   20

Use your strengths   21

The offer   21

Go for a win-win solution   22

Closing the deal   23

2. DEFINING NEGOTIATION

What is Negotiation?   **27**

Explaining negotiation   27

3. COMMUNICATION-WHAT ARE YOU TRYING TO SAY?

The Importance of Communication   31

4. THE ART OF PERSUASION-CHANGING MINDS

Persuasion Skills in negotiation   35

5. DEALING WITH PEOPLE-DEVELOPING YOUR INTERPERSONAL SKILLS

The People factor   41

Perception   42

Emotion   43

Communication   44

The main problems   44

6. TECHNIQUES USED IN NEGOTIATION

Approaches to Negotiation   49

General   49

Identifying terms and conditions of negotiations 51

Variables in negotiation 51

---

7. PREPARING FOR NEGOTIATIONS

The Importance of Preparation **55**

Consider what types of negotiations you are preparing for 55

List all the issues 56

Gather information 56

Review past negotiations 56

Consider your position if negotiations fail 56

Assess the relative strengths and weaknesses of your position 57

Decide what concessions you are prepared to make 57

Determine your strongest arguments 57

Determine your attitude 58

Make an agenda 58

Other people 59

How are you seen in negotiations?   59

Setting objectives in negotiation   60

Timing of negotiations   60

The structure of a meeting   60

8. DURING NEGOTIATIONS

In the Thick of It.   **65**

Tactics   65

Specific variables   65

Reward   66

Threat of punishment   66

Legitimacy   66

Confidence   66

The key principles of negotiation   66

Setting sights high   67

Finding out the other persons full intentions   67

Keeping all factors in mind   67

Keeping a look out for further variables   68

The initial stance of parties   68

Going for the quick kill   68

Taking a more flexible approach   68

Bridge building   69

Minimizing concessions   70

The use of techniques   71

Use of silence   71

Summarizing frequently   71

Note taking   72

9. The Dirty Tricks Department

What to Do in the face of Dirty Tricks   **75**

Some common dirty tricks   75
Deliberate deception   76
Psychological warfare   76

Positional pressure tactics 77

Extreme demands 78
Escalation of demands 79

10. REACHING AN AGREEMENT

The All Important Agreement 83

The record of agreement 83

The importance of communication 85

11. REFLECTING ON EXPERIENCE

Looking Back and Learning. 87

The main issues 87

The principles summarized 87

Conclusion and Summary of the Book

Case studies 91
Glossary of terms 109
Index 111

ACKNOWLEDGEMENTS

Thanks is given to all those who have assisted with the writing of this book during the last year. It has been a difficult process and the final text was completed after many hours of negotiation!

Foreword

This brief introduction to the process of negotiating was the result of myself being unable to find a satisfactory text which would serve as an introduction for the many students which I teach.

Quite often people hear the word negotiation and immediately envisage a room with a group of people sitting round, each trying to get what they want out of a situation and defeating the others. Of course, negotiation is usually nothing of the sort. We negotiate in all sorts of situations, from the family, to business and employment and in many other areas. The important thing to remember is that the fundamental techniques underpinning negotiations are the same whatever the situation. Clear objectives, a well worked out strategy, knowledge of the variables involved, patience, a knowledge of the other side and flexibility are key elements of any negotiation.

Having read numerous books on the subject, I came to understand that if you get too immersed in the topic, you will end up with your head spinning, thoroughly confused. None of us are supermen or women and, to be quite frank, all you need to conduct successful negotiations is an outline knowledge of what elements are required during the process and also experience to back up the theory.

This brief text should help you enormously in the process of acquiring effective negotiation techniques.

David Blanchard.

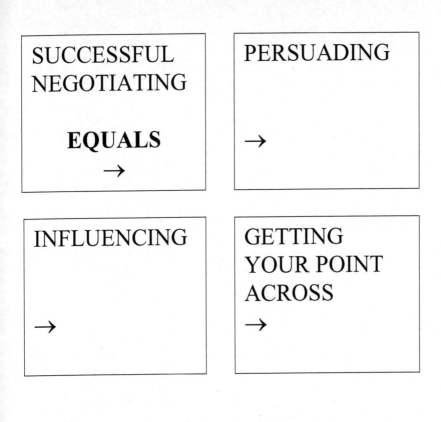

| SUCCESSFUL NEGOTIATING

EQUALS
→ | PERSUADING

→ |
|---|---|
| INFLUENCING

→ | GETTING YOUR POINT ACROSS

→ |
| LISTENING

COMPROMISE | REACHING AGREEMENT

KEEPING TO AGREEMENT |

THE STEPPING STONES TO SUCCESSFUL NEGOTIATION

1. EFFECTIVE NEGOTIATING TECHNIQUES

A SUMMARY

1

A Summary of Effective Negotiating Techniques

Below are outlined some of the key variables in successful negotiation.

Successful negotiating techniques

Negotiating is a part of everyday life, but in business it's absolutely critical to your success. Poor negotiation can cripple a company just as quickly as losing key customers. While most negotiating strategies seem like common sense, it's not uncommon for people to get caught up in the emotion of the moment and ignore their basic instincts. Emotion, luck and magic have no place in a successful negotiation. It takes an iron gut, homework, street smarts and unblinking discipline. These keys will unlock your ability to get the best deal possible under any circumstances.

Preparation is Key

Know about the party you're negotiating with so you can capitalize on your strengths and the party's weaknesses. If, for example, you are a buyer for a company then make sure you are thoroughly familiar with the product or service that will be the subject of the negotiation. If the other party senses you are weak on such details, you may be a prime target for a bluff or another technique designed to create anxiety and uncertainty. Psychology play's a crucial role in your ability to make the most of the other party's lack of preparation and anticipate their next move.

Before you start the negotiation, ensure that the other party is fully empowered to make binding commitments. You don't want to find yourself in a position where you believe you've struck a deal, only to discover that your agreement must be approved by someone higher in the chain of command.

Have a Strategy

There are basic principles that apply to every negotiation. Always have something to give away without hurting your negotiating position. Watch for clues such as body movement, speech patterns and reactions to what you say. Be prepared to suspend or cancel negotiations if you feel things are getting nowhere or the other party seems stuck in their position. Indicate your reluctance to continue under those conditions and make the other side wonder if you are ever coming back. If they are on the hook to cut a deal, they will feel the pressure to move. Be patient even if the other party isn't. This can be difficult for those with a passion for instant gratification, but the last thing you want is for the other party to think you're under the gun to finish quickly.

Once an offer is made, you should expect an acceptance or rejection of your offer, or a counter offer that keeps the negotiation open. If your offer is rejected and you are asked to submit a new and better offer, do not fall into that trap. That would be tantamount to negotiating with yourself, and you should never do this. If the last offer on the table is yours, always insist on a counteroffer to force the other party to move his/her position before you make another offer.

Use your strengths

Establish a strong foundation early in the process by demonstrating your knowledge and expertise of the negotiation subject matter. This may intimidate those on the other side and put them on their heels before they've a chance to establish their own credibility. Playing catch-up in a tough negotiation can be challenging, so it's much better to take the initiative and steer the process in the direction you want.

The Offer

An offer is more than just a monetary amount or some other deal. It must encompass all of the elements of the bargain and will normally comprise the basis for a contract that formalizes the agreement. If you make an offer without nailing down all of the specifics, you may find out later that there was no meeting of the minds with the other party.

To avoid misunderstandings, offers should be presented in writing and include all elements of the deal. It's a good idea to keep notes containing the rationale for each offer. While these notes won't be disclosed to the other party, they will prove to be invaluable should things go awry and you need to restart negotiations. Part of the process is benefiting from lessons learned and refining your approach and technique. If you work for a company or the government, those notes are usually required to document the negotiated outcome and complete the contract file.

Go For a Win-Win Solution

Throughout the negotiation, try to determine what you believe to be an acceptable outcome for the other party. It may be a combination of different things that aren't necessarily tied solely to price. For example, the delivery date may be the most important thing to the other party, while product quality may be your primary driver.

Understanding the other side's priorities is just as important as understanding your own, so figure out what you would do if you were in his shoes. When constructing your offers, attempt to satisfy some of his priorities if doing so doesn't weaken your overall position. Be prepared to give up the little things in exchange for the big things you don't want to concede. Know your limits and how far you're willing to go on all aspects of the deal.

While you have the power to influence the negotiation process in your favor, your goal should be to secure a good deal without extracting the last pound of flesh from the other party. This is especially true if you will be negotiating with the same party on a recurring basis.

The most effective negotiators are professionals who know their business and don't let personalities and irrational behavior interfere with their mission. They are capable of making the other party believe they got the best deal they could under the circumstances.

Closing the Deal

Successful negotiation is like horse-trading in that it requires a sense of timing, creativity, keen awareness and the ability to anticipate the other party's next move. Negotiation is also like chess in that each move should be designed to set up not only your next move, but several moves down the line. Generally, your moves should get progressively smaller, and you can expect the same from the other party.

Always have the endgame in mind as you plot your strategy, and be prepared at some point to split the remaining difference. It's almost inevitable when the parties are close but can't seem to make that last leap to a single number. It's completely arbitrary, but it gets the job done. That's why all the offers leading up to that point are so important: they will set the stage for the final handshake.

The above techniques, preparation, strategy, using your strengths, considering the offer and closing the deal and ensuring that you go for a win-win situation constitute the essential elements of any negotiations, whatever the context and if you are aware of these as you go you should ensure a successful outcome.

This book leads the reader through all of the essential areas of negotiation and it is hoped that the reader will gain a clear insight into the processes and emerge a more skilled negotiator.

****

2. DEFINING NEGOTIATION

WHEN YOU NEGOTIATE WHAT DO YOU WANT TO ACHIEVE?

2

What is Negotiation?

Explaining negotiation

There seems to be a lot of mystique attached to the word negotiation. Indeed, many people are afraid of the connotations attached to the word. However, everyone negotiates in some aspect of their life. It is not something that only certain people do. Negotiation is, fundamentally, a communication skill and one that is underpinned by the process of persuasion. One party tries to persuade the other to accept their point of view or to reach a point where each side is satisfied with the outcome.

Negotiation is concerned with the relationship between two parties where the needs of both are largely in balance. There are many times when you will be persuaded to do something, such as buy a new car or to do something on behalf of your company.

Essentially:

The balance of need of either party effectively defines the process of negotiation.

To be an effective negotiator, it is essential that you learn something about the process of negotiation and the skills inherent within that process. The circumstances calling for negotiation are many, including selling, buying, contractual negotiations such as employment or other organizational matters. However, in a great number of situations you need to be in possession of certain skills in order to be able to influence the outcome in a way which suits you. That is what the rest of this brief introduction to negotiation will concentrate on. How to communicate and persuade others to adopt a position which is suitable to you.

****

3. COMMUNICATION

WHAT ARE YOU TRYING TO SAY AND HOW DO YOU SAY IT?

3

The Importance of Communication

As we stated, many people are intrigued by the process of negotiation. However, what is it that makes the process of negotiation so complicated and why do people wish to acquire the necessary skills to be able to conduct this process effectively?

Often, there are many complex twists and turns to discussions and the outcomes of such discussions cannot be simple. There are so many different angles to certain discussions that to achieve a satisfactory outcome to all parties concerned is very difficult indeed. Essentially there is a competitive, or adversarial, aspect to negotiations. Each person involved wishes to ensure that they obtain the best result for themselves. However, this particular aspect must be controlled, in successful negotiation, so that each party involved can feel that they have achieved. If this is not the case, then what we have is not negotiation but outright confrontation.

The skilled negotiator will understand that the outcome of discussions must be felt to be equitable by all even if in fact a party is left without the result they desired. In short, there is a very subtle psychology underpinning negotiation. This has to be understood as a prerequisite to successful and effective negotiation.

There is a vital element underpinning the whole process of influencing others-that is the art of **communication**. It is absolutely necessary to ensure that what you are saying is crystal clear to the other side. If it is not you will never succeed in negotiation. Communication can be viewed in several lights, there is the process of everyday communication, which involves those we interact with on a regular basis, or there is communication in the field of business, which is where most, but by no means all, communication takes place. However, the following points must be borne in mind:

- If what you are saying is unclear to the other side then the process of negotiation will run into problems

- If you are not exact or precise in what you are saying then you will run into problems

- If you jargonise then the other side will not understand and you will create problems

Essentially, clarity is of the utmost importance. There are two sides to this. The first is that if people are unclear about what it is you are saying, what point you are trying to make, then you cannot hope to persuade them which is the next vital step in negotiating. In addition, you yourself will lose the thread of what it is you are talking about, or what you are trying to achieve and will put yourself in a position where you will lose whatever ground you have gained.

****

4. THE ART OF PERSUASION

HOW DO YOU CHANGE
PEOPLES MINDS AND BRING
THEM AROUND TO YOUR WAY
OF THINKING?

4

Persuasion Skills in Negotiation

It is very easy for communication to end up being unpersuasive. This very much depends on the approach taken toward the other person and whether or not their point of view is taken into consideration. People will not be persuaded if they think that someone is trying to get one over on them. Instead they will close up and be defensive and negotiations will go nowhere.

Generally, you have to start by thinking of the thought processes involved when considering another persons request for action. Generally, this process is one that is seen to move through a number of stages:

- The other persons need to feel important and respected
- Consideration of the others needs
- The need to feel that the proposition being put forward will be of benefit
- The need to understand the facts
- The need to understand the pitfalls
- The need to understand what to do
- The desire, or otherwise, to approve what is being put forward.

This is part of the weighing up process, assessing the good against the bad and attempting to come to a decision.

Any attempt at communication that results in an unsatisfactory response in any of the above stages is unlikely to end in agreement. This is because the process of "frustration" has occurred and there will be delays whilst problems are sorted out and points are clarified. Among the many techniques of persuasion in existence, matching the persons decision making thoughts and describing your own case in a way that reflects that, are key.

Successful outcomes do not always arise from the initial contact between those involved in the decision making process. Because of the complexity and the fact that there may be frustration in the process, then other meetings may be necessary. It is essential to think ahead and try to see where you went wrong. Ensure that you are aware of the processes as described and that you can analyze each stage and prepare yourself for the next round.

If persuasion is to succeed it is necessary to tackle communication with a clear eye on the listener and their point of view. The whole approach must be seen to be acceptable, must come over as acceptable.

There are several factors which join to make a person's manner acceptable:

- Projection

- Empathy

Essentially, projection means the way we come over to other people. When people are in a position of stress they quite often project, as a way of offloading on to other people. Empathy means the ability to understand another, to put yourself in their place and to understand how they feel and how you would feel if you were there. The other person must feel that you are empathizing with them.

It is worth, at this point, taking a look at the different types of communication, and communicators, each with varying degrees of empathy and thus success:

- There is the person who is very aggressive and oversensitive. They quite often win arguments but they project without empathy. This becomes self-defeating and closes up others, who become very defensive.

- There is the person who has very little interest in the whole process and conveys that. This lack of commitment leads to a lack of conclusion

- There is the weak communicator. They come over nice and well-meaning but do not achieve a lot. Basically, they will take the side of the other party to the negotiations and they achieve little

- The ideal communicator has a creative understanding of the listener and is often a sensitive person, being empathetic with others. As we stated, being seen to have understood the others point of view is essential to successful outcomes in negotiations.

Only when someone is persuaded in principle towards a particular course of action will they be interested in moving on to the stage of making a deal.

****

5. DEALING WITH PEOPLE- DEVELOPING YOUR INTERPERSONAL SKILLS

5

The People factor

In chapter one, we discussed the main elements underpinning negotiation. We defined negotiation and saw that the crucial elements in the process of negotiation are communication and persuasion. We will be exploring communication further in this chapter.

However, *negotiators are people first.* When negotiating, it is easy to forget that the "other side" are people too. People have emotions, deeply held beliefs and values, they often come from different backgrounds and have different opinions. They are as unpredictable as you are.

A working relationship where understanding, respect and trust have been built up can help the negotiation process enormously. Peoples desire to feel good about their selves, and their concern for what others will think about them, can often make them more sensitive to another negotiators interests.

On the other hand, people can be afraid and angry and also feel frustrated and hostile. They can misinterpret what you say. Misunderstanding can reinforce prejudice and rational negotiation can break down. The purpose of the game then becomes one of scoring points and apportioning blame.

Failing to deal with others sensitively and recognize that we are all prone to human reactions can be disastrous for negotiation. It is therefore essential that, whatever else you are doing at any point in the negotiation process, you ask yourself "am I paying enough attention to the people factor"?

It is useful to focus on the people factor by breaking it down into three categories:

- Perception

- Emotion

- Communication

Perception

Often the problem lies not only in objective reality but also in peoples heads. The difference between your thinking and theirs. Fears, even if ill-founded are quite often real fears and need to be dealt with. Hopes, even if unrealistic, cause conflict. It is the reality as each side sees it that constitutes the problem in a negotiation, recognizing that this opens the way for a solution.

- Put yourself in their shoes

- Don't deduce their intentions from your fears

- Avoid blaming them for your problem

- Make perceptions explicit and discuss them

- Look for opportunities to act consistently with another's perceptions

- Involve people in the process

- Face-saving, make your proposals consistent with their values

Emotion

In a negotiation feelings may be more important than words. Parties may be more ready for battle than for co-operatively working out a solution to a common problem. People often come to a negotiation feeling that the stakes are high and feel threatened. Emotions on the one side generate emotions on the other.

Fear may breed anger and anger fear. Emotions may quickly bring negotiation to a deadlock.

- Recognize and understand emotions, yours and theirs

- Make emotions explicit and acknowledge them as legitimate

- Allow the other side to let off steam

- Don't react emotionally to emotional outbursts

- Use symbolic gestures

Communication

As we have seen, without communication there is no negotiation. Negotiation is a process of communicating back and forth for the purpose of reaching a joint decision. Communication is never an easy thing, even for people who have an enormous background of shared values and experience. Where two people are in a situation where suspicion or hostility are common feelings it is not surprising that communication is poor.

There are three main problems:

- The negotiators may not be talking to each other, or at least not in a way to be understood.

- Even if you are talking clearly and directly to them, they may not be hearing you.

- Misunderstanding.

To overcome these problems we need to:

- Listen actively and acknowledge what is being said

- Speak to be understood

- Speak about yourself, not them

- Speak for a purpose.

Although these techniques for dealing with problems of perception, emotion and communication usually work well, the best time for handling the people factor is before they become problems. This means building a personal and organizational relationship with the other side, and structuring the negotiation in ways that separate the substantive problem from the relationship.

****

6. TECHNIQUES USED IN NEGOTIATION

6

Approaches and Techniques Used in Negotiation

Negotiation is not a process whereby one party feels that they must win at all costs.

General points

The process of negotiation needs to be understood clearly. There is obviously more to negotiation than just sitting down and agreeing or disagreeing. Otherwise, books would not be written on the subject and people would not go to expensive seminars. As my son said to me, "why do you need to write a book to help people make decisions"? My response was that the more complicated the subject matter and the greater the potential losses, the harder it is for all parties to the process to come to an agreement.

Coming to an agreement can be seen in the light of what is known as "win-win" dealing. It is absolutely fundamental to the process of negotiation that both the parties involved end up feeling satisfied that a deal appropriate to their needs has been done and that the end result is reasonably acceptable to them. As we have discussed, each side must also feel that they have been understood by the other parties to the negotiations and there has not been an attempt to "rip them off".

This is not negotiation this is aggression and hostility and bullying the other side into submission. Negotiation is a process of give and take, flexibility and meeting somewhere outside of what was originally desired.

We need to look at some of the finer points of the processes underlying win-win negotiations:

- The approach should be one of seeking common ground, as opposed to trying to get your way on everything

- You need to show that you empathize with the other parties to the negotiations rather than merely objecting to them

- Be ready to compromise

- Discussions within a negotiation framework must encompass debate that goes to and fro rather than being conducted within a rigid framework

- Discussions within a negotiating framework should consist of questioning-and listening-rather than mere statements of one's case

- Be open, disclosing appropriate information to the other side rather than being defensive and secretive

Negotiation is not a process whereby one party feels that they must win at all costs.

- The emphasis should be on building relationships with parties to a negotiation rather than instilling bad feelings

- The aim in all negotiations is that of agreement. Quite often the end result is one of stalemate because of lack of understanding and intransigence.

Identifying terms and conditions of negotiations

The key point when conducting negotiations is that the outset of negotiation is the process of identification of actual terms and conditions of whatever deal you are involved in. The arranging and agreement of terms and conditions then has to take place. Once this has taken place you can then move onto the actual discussions.

When you reach a crucial stage in negotiations, where a persons mind has been influenced and he or she has been persuaded of your case, and agreement in principle begins to emerge, it is time to begin to think "on what basis will the other party agree?" At this point it is time to consider detail and for each party to decide whether all points of the deal suits them. Total satisfaction will probably not result but the balance must be right.

Variables in negotiation

Underlying all negotiations are the variables which must be considered. Variables are the basic raw materials of negotiation.

There are often many variables and for certain when negotiating you will need an idea of the nature and type and number of variables and also an idea of the importance. The more variables that there are, and the more difficult to rank, or prioritize, the more complex the negotiation becomes. In addition, human interactions inherently complicate the negotiation.

Having considered the variables and ranked them in order of importance, then it is time to consider what exactly brings success in the process of negotiation. Success rests on three factors:

- What you do

- How you go about it

- Preparation

The first two elements are wholly dependent on preparation. Sound preparation can give you the all important "edge" which gives you a head start in comparison with the next person.

****

7. PREPARING FOR NEGOTIATIONS

SETTING THE SCENE

7

The Importance of Preparation

Being well prepared breeds confidence. Appearing confident will be seen by others as competence. Preparation itself may be just a few moments thought prior to negotiation or it may mean a few hours with colleagues. Whatever, it is of vital importance if you wish to maintain an edge.

When preparing:

- Consider others involved in the process

- Consider your own position in relation to others

Consider what type of negotiations you are preparing for:

- Win/win or lose/lose

- Bilateral negotiations or Multilateral negotiations?

- Must agreement be reached?

- Will the agreement be enforceable?

- Will the other person be involved in the agreements implementation?

- Where and how will the negotiations be held?

List all the issues

- What are the main issues?

- Are there wider issues involved?

- How do the issues interrelate?

- What are the interests behind the issues?

- What exactly do you want?

Gather information about the subject-about the other persons position/interests.

Consider what information you need to offer during the negotiation and what you might expect in exchange.

Review past negotiations with the other person.

- What lessons can be learnt?

Consider your position if the negotiation fails

- What action will you take?

Assess the relative strengths and weaknesses of your positions

- How much do you need the other person's co-operation and vice versa?

- What are your alternatives and what are the other persons?

- Whose side is time on? What deadlines do you both have?

With regard to all the issues at stake, decide on your:

- Opening offer/ demand
- Realistic optimum target

- Satisfaction level

- Walk away point or bottom line.

Decide what concessions you are prepared to make

- Consider the cost to you and value to the other person

- What order you will offer them in

Determine what your strongest arguments are in making your case

- Decide on your strategy and tactics for conducting the negotiation.

What attitude will you adopt?

Friendly, co-operative, informal, formal rigid etc. Take account of the circumstances, the other person and your own personality.

- How much time have you got?

- How much authority do you have, want to have, don't have?

- If you are negotiating as a team, what role is each member taking?

Put yourself in the other person shoes

- What are his needs?

- What does he want?
- Review the entire checklist through his/her eyes.

Make an agenda for the meeting, including time and place

- Discuss it with the other person and be prepared to be flexible.

Rehearse if time and importance justify

Be prepared to be flexible during the negotiation, departing if necessary from the prepared position.

Other people

Negotiations take place with all sorts of people. They may or may not be known to you personally. You need to ask certain fundamental questions:

- What role or intentions does the other have?

- What needs do they have?

- What problems will they raise during the course of negotiations?

- What, if any, objections will they raise?

- Do they have the authority to decide things or must they defer to others?

Each specific situation will raise different issues, but the principle of thinking through how people may handle something is similar in each case. Do not overlook this, or assume familiarity makes it unnecessary. Even with people you know and deal with regularly, such analysis may pay dividends.

How you are seen in negotiations

The other party in negotiations is yourself and how you are perceived by others is very important. If you appear professional and competent you will gain respect. If you appear flustered and convey the impression that you do not have control of the situation then you will very quickly lose respect.. Underpinning the way you appear to others is confidence and this can only really be gained if you are prepared.

Setting out objectives

It is essential that you have objectives set out very clearly in your own mind. You need to identify and set specific objectives, which can be measured. You need to have a clear set of priorities and they need to be very clearly linked to the variables involved. You need to understand your attitude to the variables and how far you may wish to compromise around each.

Timing of negotiations

It is very important to consider timing. For example, are you intent on achieving everything at once or are you prepared to wait until a satisfactory outcome is achieved? If you have a clear set of objectives, and understand the variables involved, then you can begin to get a clear idea of the time frame within which you want to achieve your goals.

The structure of a meeting

Structure means the actual shape and style, thus form, of the meeting. Structure includes everything that helps the meeting along and avoids muddles. Account needs to be taken of likely timing of the meeting. Your order of sequence and priority must fit within the duration of the meeting. You will need to be very clear about priorities and which are primary matters in negotiation, i.e., matters of the most importance and also secondary matters.

Remember, preparation is of vital importance and without effective groundwork you may lose that all important edge and thus not gain what you want.

****

8. DURING NEGOTIATIONS

IN THE THICK OF IT!

8

In The Thick of It!

Negotiations are generally quite complicated and it is essential that meetings are managed effectively. Negotiations involve two separate processes which interact together:

- Tactics of negotiations

- The behavior of each of the negotiators

Tactics

Occasionally, the balance of power is very definitely slanted in one parties favor. In this case the result is often in no doubt. However, in most situations which involve negotiation the balance of power is dispersed and certain acts are required to swing the balance. Both sides bring the power to negotiate to the table. Power can mean the following:

Specific variables

The most obvious sources of power are the specific variables that are most important to a negotiation. These can be anything, from finance to commodities. Variables can be both tangible and intangible and usually both are involved.

Reward

This is something that you can offer to the other party if they can be influenced. If you have something that the other wants then they will listen.

Threats of punishment

This is where there is an apparent intention not to give something that the other side wants.

Legitimacy

Legitimacy means the factual evidence. It can swing the balance without much argument. This can be a written quote from another party which may prove that the point you are making to the demands being made are legitimate through someone else's perception of price.

Confidence

Confidence in negotiations will almost certainly arise from initial preparation. It is hard to deal with someone who appears to be very confident and you wish to ensure that the confident person is you.

The key principles of negotiation

There are four guiding principles which combine to help the process of negotiation.

These are as follows:

- Set your sights as high as possible

- Find out the other persons intentions

- Keep the entirety of the factors in play in mind

- Keep looking for further variables

Setting sights high

Always aim high. You can always work your way downwards from the highest point if you want. However, it is difficult to trade up.

Finding out the other persons full intentions

The more complete the picture of the other person the better. The more that you know about their requirements the easier it is to decide exactly what you are going to give, or otherwise. You need as much information about the other person as possible and quite often this comes from prior preparation.

Keeping all factors in mind

As the picture builds up so the process becomes more complex. It is easy as you plan ahead to forget some of the issues that you need to keep in mind. You need to have a clear head, make notes and to plan ahead as you go.

Keeping a look out for further variables

You need to remain flexible at all times. Avoid getting locked into previous plans. The good negotiator is quick on their feet. Sometimes, what happens is very much along the lines that you expected. However, some fine-tuning is always necessary.

The process of negotiation assumes a balance. Although participants are often initially far apart on the scale and there is a perceived imbalance, both parties will settle on something which is assumed reasonable. This is why people accept. In very few instances do parties walk away from the negotiating table feeling aggrieved.

THE INITIAL STANCE OF PARTIES

The initial stance refers to the starting point that each party begins with. There are a number of options:

Going for the quick kill

This is the extreme end of the scale where one party says to another "take it or leave it" This is a very hard approach and is difficult to deal with although does not rule out negotiations. Anyone starting from this point obviously thinks that they are in a position of power to begin with.

Taking a more flexible approach

At the other end of the scale the conversation might begin on a more flexible note, such as "lets talk about what you want and see if we can't arrive at a compromise". This is more suitable when the negotiators do not have a particularly strong case and wish to arrive at a reasonable solution.

It is said that the higher the opening stance the better the final deal achieved. It is difficult to negotiate down from nothing and an initially extreme stance can throw the other off balance. Ultimately, the first phase of negotiations is only a clarification of initial stances. Soon after, a better and less extreme point is adopted by each in the process which allows for negotiations proper to begin.

Bridge building

There is certainly a need to develop a rapport as the process proceeds. This brings the parties closer together and enables the other parties to the process to see your point of view. There are a number of key approaches to bridge building:

- Open the discussions on a neutral subject

- Show respect for the other party and the process of negotiations

- Refer back, if necessary, to past agreements. This helps reinforce persuasion.

- Be clear about complicated and complex issues

The above tactics during negotiations put the process on the basis of reason and flexibility rather than the proverbial brick wall. Adopting these tactics results in bridges being constructed throughout the process.

It is important to ask questions of the other parties to the process and really be clear as to their intentions and what they mean. It is at this stage that you may wish to begin trading concessions. You should avoid giving anything away early on in the process. This is very important indeed.

Never give a concession. Appear to be trading it reluctantly. You want to be seen by the other parties as driving a hard bargain. If you don't then you will not be taken seriously. It is important, in this context to optimize your concessions and minimize the other parties. Optimizing your concessions means:

- Stressing the cost to you

- Exaggerating, but maintaining a certain credibility

- Refer to a major problem that a concession made by you will solve

- Imply that you are making a major concession.

Minimizing concessions

This means:

- Do not overdo thanks. Don't be too profuse
- Depreciating them, minimizing the value
- Treating them as having very little value

- Taking them for granted
- Devaluing them by implying that you already have what's on offer anyway
- Denying any value

Concessions are either minimized or optimized as deemed appropriate. The skilled negotiator will trade a concession which in fact will cost them little. It has, though, an implied value which brings a relatively more valuable concession in return from the other side. It is this difference in value that gives an edge.

The use of techniques

There are other techniques which are very important in negotiation.

These are:

Use of silence

Keeping quiet can be as powerful as speaking. Silence can unnerve the other side and lead them to say something or give something away. It is difficult to maintain complete silence but inevitably something will give.

Summarizing frequently

Negotiations can sometimes be very complicated. They often involve the juggling of a number of variables. It is very easy to lose direction. Never be afraid to recap on the process or to summarize in order to regain your thoughts.

Note taking

This also will help keep complex negotiations on track. Never put yourself in a position where you have to grope to remember what was said. This may call into question your level of expertise. Taking notes will act as an aide memoir and ensure that you have all the facts at your fingertips.

You should remember that negotiation involves adversaries. Both parties want the best and both will try to get the best. Maintain neutrality as much as possible. Concentrate and keep ahead of the process. Be in charge of yourself and the process as a whole. Run the conversation in a way that you want and not a way that the other wants. Get off to a good start and remain conscious of what the other party wants and is trying to achieve.

****

9. THE DIRTY TRICKS DEPARTMENT

9

What to Do in The Face of Dirty Tricks

We have so far assumed that negotiations are, in the main, principled and reasonable. However, there will be times when you are dealing with people who have other motives and will try to pull one over on you. What do you do then?

There are numerous tactics and tricks that people will use to try to get the better of you and swing the balance their way. The most obvious are lies and psychological abuse and also various pressure tactics.. The standard response to these tactics is to put up with them. However, you might make a decision never to deal with these people again. For now, you hope for the best and stay quiet. Most people will respond in this way, in the hope that if you appease the other side they won't ask for more. Sometimes this works. However, more often it fails as you have shown a weakness that will, or can be exploited. If you know history, then you will know that Neville Chamberlain went down this road with Adolf Hitler. One year later, Hitler declared war and World War 11 started.

The other response to underhand tactics is to respond in kind. If they start very high with their demands, you offer very low, if they are deceptive and employ mind games so do you. If they use threats and counter-threats so do you. And so on. All too often negotiations break off and nothing is achieved except hostility.

To ensure that you avoid these kind of negotiating tactics you need to lay down rules, to negotiate about the negotiating process itself. There are a number of steps that you can take where the other side seems to be using underhand tactics. The first is to recognize the tactic and raise it as an issue immediately, bringing it out into the open. Question the tactic's legitimacy and desirability and negotiate over it. You have to know what is going on to recognize it and to challenge it. Recognizing, for example, that the other side is attacking you on a personal level to try to undermine you and make you feel uncomfortable, impairing your judgment, may well frustrate the attempt.

The most important purpose of bring up the tactic explicitly is to give you a chance to negotiate about the rules of the game, letting the other side see that you wish to avoid spoiling tactics and attempt to reach an objective reasonable agreement. basically, insist on using objective criteria, avoiding the personal.

As a last resort, in the face of dirty dealing, you can walk out of the negotiations altogether. make it clear why you are walking out which should serve to focus the other sides minds. Say something like" its my distinct impression that you're not really interested in reaching a fair agreement, here is my phone number ring me back when you decide to negotiate fairly, otherwise, see you in court" (or something like this).

Some common dirty tricks

There are a number of dirty tricks but the most common seem to be deliberate deception, psychological warfare and positional pressure tactics. Lets look at all three in turn.

Deliberate deception

This usually consists of misrepresentation about facts, authority or intentions. You might be negotiating the price of a car and listen to wild claims about mileage, one lady owner etc. The best position to be in is to know the facts beforehand, if possible, and challenge wild claims or deliberate lies. Don't attack the person but challenge the facts. The most important lesson in negotiations, especially when they get tricky, is to keep to the objectives, don't turn your challenges into personal attacks. If you are not in a position to check facts and wild claims then you should give yourself breathing space to go away and check. If the other side are confident in their assertions they won't mind this. If they are not then you know that misrepresentation is happening and you should ask the other side to back up their claims.

Psychological warfare

Some people absolutely revel in this and will always try to gain advantage by use of various ploys, for example as we have seen, personal attacks. These tactics are designed to make you feel uncomfortable and stressed out and to want to end negotiations early.

You need to consider where the negotiations are taking place: your place or theirs or on a neutral territory. Contrary to expectations, offering to meet on the other sides territory can help to move things along by putting them at ease and being more open to suggestion. If necessary, it also makes it easier to walk out. However, if you do let the other side choose the environment then think carefully about what this entails and any advantages this may confer.

In addition to manipulating the physical environment, there are also other ways to use verbal and non-verbal communication to make you feel uncomfortable. They can comment on your clothes or general appearance, thereby personalizing things straight away. They can attack your status by making you wait for them or by interrupting the negotiations and talking to others. they can imply that you are ignorant of facts or make you repeat yourself. Avoidance of eye contact is a common ploy. In each case, recognizing the tactic will help to nullify it's effect.

Threats are also very common in negotiation. Threats of one sort of another lead to pressure. A classic example of the use of threats is in trade union negotiations. The use of threats here quite often means that the unions close ranks, or the employers, and things go nowhere. Good negotiators rarely resort to threats, they don't need to as they are experienced enough to realize the overall effect.

Positional pressure tactics

This kind of bargaining tactic is designed to manipulate the situation so that only one side can effectively make concessions. usually, it consists of one side refusing to negotiate altogether, for example a lawyer stating that "we will see you in court". What can be done in the face of this approach?

The first thing is that you should see this as a possible negotiating ploy. The person who is stating that they will not negotiate is attempting to use this as a bargaining chip, giving them an advantage straight away to obtain some concession on substance. Another ploy is to set preconditions for negotiations. The best thing to do is to talk about their refusal to negotiate, communicate either directly or through third parties. Don't attack them for their refusal but find out the reasons for not wanting to negotiate, what are their worries or concerns.

Extreme demands

Negotiators will sometimes start with extreme demand, offering a ridiculously low price which is far below the worth of what is being sold. The goal is to lower your expectations. Bringing this tactic to their attention will seek to undermine their approach. Ask for a justification for their position. More often than not they won't be able to justify it and will look ridiculous.

Escalation of demands

A negotiator may raise one of his demands for every concession he makes on another. He may also reopen issues you thought had been agreed. The benefits of this tactic lie in decreasing the overall concession and in the psychological effect of making you want to agree quickly before he raises any more of his demands

The best way to counter this is to bring it to their attention and, rather than being bounced into anything call for a break in negotiations whilst you consider the offers.

In the final analysis you need to be aware of dirty tricks and be able to counter them. Don't be bullied and pushed into anything. Always stay calm and objective and let the other side know that you won't be rattled and won't give away anything that you don't want to give away.

****

10. REACHING AN AGREEMENT

ARRIVING AT AN ACCEPTABLE AGREEMENT

10

Reaching Agreement

Having established the framework for negotiations and prepared yourself thoroughly and, hopefully sidestepped the dirty tricks, if there are any, it is necessary to consider the art of reaching an agreement and having all sides clearly recognizing the agreement and, most importantly, sticking by it.

The record of agreement

It is important to bear in mind that some negotiations are informal and require no record of agreement. However, other negotiations are formal and it is essential that the agreement reached is documented and understood by all parties to the process.

Agreements in negotiations are usually contractual. Verbal agreements are contracts. Written agreements are binding. Therefore, it is essential that:

- Contractual situations are communicated clearly and reinforced if necessary, with no possibility of misunderstanding
- The contract enhances the relationship involved, if necessary on a continuing basis

- The contract allows the progressing and securing of agreement to proceed effectively and promptly.

Contractual arrangements need to make clear:

- The basis of the agreement

- The terminology to be used by both parties

- All elements of timing

- The procedures, documentation and administration involved

- All financial matters in detail

A contract may cause problems if it also causes surprises. Producing a hefty document for signature when there was no mention of it in the first place can cause upset. You need to make matters such as the outcome leading to a binding contract very clear from the outset.

The introduction of a contract, or the fact that there will be a contract has to be handled in the right way. Right at the outset you need to introduce the concept of a contract. You need to ensure that the details are crystal clear. Ensure that any figures and timing in the contract are clear to all parties. Check and double check the understanding.

Document carefully your side of the arrangements and ask for their confirmation that they have understood. If you deal with contractual matters in the right way then there should be minimal problems. However, what if the other party fails to comply with the contract? There are a number of options:

- Stick to the exact wording of the contract insisting that the other side do so

- Negotiate a compromise

- Make exceptions

Whatever you do, it is important not to allow the other party to deviate from the contract without recognition on your part.

The importance of communication

It can be seen that communication is once again at the heart of reaching an agreement, ensuring that all involved clearly understand the agreement and that there are no problems once contracts are signed. However, it is vital that you receive others confirmation that all is understood and that they intend to abide by the agreement thereafter.

****

11 REFLECTING ON EXPERIENCE

HOW IT ALL WENT AND LESSONS LEARNT

11

Looking Back and Learning

The main issues

In this final chapter, it is important to reflect on the whole process of negotiating.

Negotiation is a mixture of science and art, a dynamic interactive process and needs to be conducted in a way that is well planned and yet at the same time flexible.

To negotiate successfully you must see the process totally, take a very broad view and continue to do so through the process. This means that you must have a good grasp of the principles involved.

The principles summarized:

- Definition: negotiation is about bargaining to reach a mutually agreeable outcome. This is the win-win concept
- Never neglect preparation. Have a clear plan but remain flexible at all times
- Participants must regard each other as equals. Mutual respect is essential to both the conduct of negotiations and the outcome
- Negotiation is about discussion rather than debate

- Put your cards on the table, at least on major issues
- Patience is very important in negotiations. Delay is better than a poor outcome
- Empathy is important. The need to put yourself in the others shoes is paramount
- State objectives very clearly
- Avoid confrontation. Do not put yourself in a position that you cannot get out of and avoid rows and arguments
- Treat disagreement very carefully
- Deal with concessions progressively. What concessions have to be made, make them unwillingly and one by one
- Be realistic and do not expect perfection
- Use openness but not comprehensively. Declaring your plans may be useful to the discussion. You may want to hide the motivation behind them
- Set your sights high and settle as high as possible
- Keep up your guard
- Remain professional
- Never underestimate others
- End negotiations on a positive note.

Like any interactive process, negotiation is very dependent on a number of factors. The following are some of those factors:

- Select the right starting point. Your plan should allow for you to take the initiative and quickly get on to your agenda
- Start as high as possible then any trading can move you to a position not far below your starting point

- Never make your feelings that obvious. Negotiations are like a game of poker in that you do not want to allow the other side to see how you are feeling
- Make use of silence
- Keep a look out for early difficulties. Let a mutual rapport build up before you approach difficult issues
- Do not exaggerate facts
- Communicate very clearly. Leave nothing confused or unclear
- Be seen to go with the other persons way of doing things, at least to some degree
- Do not push too hard as this can lead to a situation where both parties are unwilling to give too much
- When you have finished negotiations, stop and conclude the matter. Do not allow further changes to what you have agreed.

There are several elements which must be avoided.

Never:
- Over-react if the outcomes of negotiations or responses are negative
- allow yourself to become over emotional. This will weaken your overall resolve
- agree to something that you really do not want.

Negotiation is underpinned by a basic list of techniques which should serve as the structure for and discussions. Experience is the most important element. From experience you can learn from mistakes and hopefully never repeat them.

Preparation is the key to successful negotiations. Many people do not prepare and then lose out in the negotiating round. Awareness of the process is equally important. If you are actively aware of the overall process then negotiations will be that much easier.

Confidence is also paramount. Planning is the starting point for confidence in negotiations. If you know what you want, have aimed high in the outset and have a plan through which you can achieve your aims then you will be confident.

****

CONCLUSION AND SUMMARY OF THE BOOK

This brief book has, hopefully, outlined the main elements in the negotiation process. There are many books out there which deal with the art of negotiation and, to be quite frank, you would need to be some kind of superman or woman to remember everything involved. This book keeps it brief.

To summarize:

What is negotiation?

There seems to be a lot of mystique attached to the word negotiation. Indeed, many people are afraid of the connotations attached to the word. However, everyone negotiates in some aspect of their life. It is not something that only certain people do. Negotiation is, fundamentally, a communication skill and one that is underpinned by the process of persuasion. One party tries to persuade the other to accept their point of view or to reach a point where each side is satisfied with the outcome.

Negotiation is concerned with the relationship between two parties where the needs of both are largely in balance. There are many times when you will be persuaded to do something, such as buy a new car or to do something on behalf of your company.

Essentially:
The balance of need of either party effectively defines the process of negotiation.

Negotiators are people first. When negotiating, it is easy to forget that the "other side" are people too. People have emotions, deeply held beliefs and values, they often come from different backgrounds and have different opinions. They are as unpredictable as you are.

A working relationship where understanding, respect and trust have been built up can help the negotiation process enormously. Peoples desire to feel good about themselves, and their concern for what others will think about them, can often make them more sensitive to another negotiators interests.

Win-Win dealing

Coming to an agreement can be seen in the light of what is known as "win-win" dealing. It is absolutely fundamental to the process of negotiation that both the parties involved end up feeling satisfied that a deal appropriate to their needs has been done and that the end result is reasonably acceptable to them. As we have discussed, each side must also feel that they have been understood by the other parties to the negotiations and there has not been an attempt to "rip them off".

> *Negotiation is not a process whereby one party feels that they must win at all costs.*

Bridge building

There is certainly a need to develop a rapport as the process proceeds. This brings the parties closer together and enables the other parties to the process to see your point of view. There are a number of key approaches to bridge building:

- Open the discussions on a neutral subject

- Show respect for the other party and the process of negotiations

- Refer back, if necessary, to past agreements. This helps reinforce persuasion.

- Be clear about complicated and complex issues

Reaching an agreement

Having established the framework for negotiations and prepared yourself thoroughly it is necessary to consider the art of reaching an agreement and having all sides clearly recognizing the agreement and, most importantly, sticking by it.

It is important to bear in mind that some negotiations are informal and require no record of agreement. However, other negotiations are formal and it is essential that the agreement reached is documented and understood by all parties to the process. Agreements in negotiations are usually contractual. Verbal agreements are contracts. Written agreements are binding.

Negotiation is a mixture of science and art, a dynamic interactive process and needs to be conducted in a way that is well planned and yet at the same time flexible.

To negotiate successfully you must see the process totally, take a very broad view and continue to do so through the process. This means that you must have a good grasp of the principles involved.

Throughout this book the emphasis has been on the fact that negotiation is a process of planning, knowing what you want, aiming high, understanding the other parties to the process,, being patient and professional and ensuring positive outcomes for yourself.

It should be clear that the process of negotiation is not some mystical and intimidating process. It is an event which has to be well structured and your objectives clear. The path to attaining your objectives is the process of planning, which should give you the necessary confidence to get what you want.

Always treat others with respect. However, do not allow your self to be put in a position where you are giving away more than you need to, or more than is desirable.

****

Case studies

The three examples outlined overleaf show particular circumstances, each with a varying degree of difficulty. The cases become progressively harder to resolve and each requires varying degrees of skills. The final case is the most difficult of all.

The first case is one where the desired outcomes of both parties are very similar. The second case demonstrates what may happen where the outcomes and the obstacles are greater within a business setting. The third case highlights the difficulties faced where complete intransigence is encountered and involves the construction and planning process.

1.

WORKPLACE NEGOTIATIONS

NEGOTIATIONS IN THE WORKPLACE

David works for a medium size advertising company and is seeking promotion to a higher paid job with better prospects. Over the past two years the company has changed shape and David has assumed a lot more responsibility and also has extra managerial responsibilities. He needs to ascertain whether or not his employer will negotiate a new position for him based on his changed job or whether they will decide to recruit outside.

The personnel director, Michael needs to ensure that the post is filled by the right person, someone who is capable. However, he also needs to ensure that money is not wasted.

David knows enough to plan for the meeting. He has considered the following:

- The nature of the new job
- His own strengths and why the company should employ him
- The package he considers appropriate

The package has plenty of variables, such as salary, car, expenses, bonuses, pensions etc.

David considers his approach to the forthcoming negotiations and what impression he will make. Too strong in this particular circumstance and he may be thought too difficult. Too soft and this may convey weakness. Therefore, it is essential that David does the following:

- Prioritize the variables

- Decide on an initial approach which will convey the correct message.

The personnel director has also prepared. He wants to be able to confirm the appointment. He has also thought through all the variables.

Both parties want something good for the company and yet are also initially adversaries. They are, however, equally matched. A win-win outcome is desirable for both. David wants to accept the post without too many regrets about the package. Michael wants him too accept, move into the post and carry on working. Therefore, the goals are not so different.

The way the two parties conduct themselves will affect the outcome. Whatever the outcome, it will not be something that just happened. It will depend on the skills of both and how they each deploy techniques involved in communication generally and negotiation in particular. The two parties will make the outcome what it is.

****

NEGOTIATING IN BUSINESS

NEGOTIATING IN BUSINESS

This case involves a medium-size publishing company, Diamond Publishing limited. Diamond publishing has had a good relationship with its printers for three years, having 90 days credit and a good scale of prices for printed matter.

However, over the last month, the printer has stated that it is changing focus and is moving towards long run journal publishing. Therefore, Diamond publishing's print contract must be terminated. The managing director of Diamond has made contact with other printers and has negotiated a deal with one, with whom he places an order after having received what seem to be favorable estimates. The estimates are based on the receipt of future work which will make the job economically worthwhile.

The work is duly finished, although it is late. When the invoices arrive for the work to the managing directors dismay they are 50% higher than the original estimate. The printer explains that the material supplied to them originally was not as specified, more work has gone into production and therefore higher costs incurred. This is the reason for the increase.

The publisher has organized a meeting with the printer to resolve the problem and to set the agenda for the future.

In this situation, the publisher stands to lose a lot of money and a potentially stable printing arrangement with preferential credit terms.

The printer stands to lose further work with the publisher. However, there may be a loss on these first jobs.

In this situation, clearly both parties must:

- Outline the possible advantages and disadvantages of severing the relationship with each other

- The publisher must try to persuade the printer that by lowering the invoice costs, both present and future, more work will come their way

The printer must plan an approach with all the variables clear. Will it try to influence the outcome of discussions by persuading the publisher that it should pay the initial higher price because of the extra work or will it accept a lower initial invoice in the light of future works.

Both parties want a win-win situation but both may wish to adopt an initial stance which is favorable to them in the short term.

There are a number of ways this could go. However, the nature and type of person that each face will be of the utmost importance in the final outcome.

Intransigence may be one possibility. In this case neither party will achieve what they wish. The process of persuasion through reasoning is very important. The laying out of ultimate objectives and the recognizing of variables underpins the negotiating strategy.

NEGOTIATING IN BUSINESS-2

This involves a housing association which wishes to develop 40 houses for people in need. The local authority in whose area the association wishes to develop has also received a request from a private builder who wishes to develop housing for sale on the site. The builder has argued that the need for low cost housing is not great and that there are many people with disposable income in the area who could pay for housing on the open market.

The local authority planners have considered the merits of each proposal and have decided that it is not so supportive of the housing associations plans. However, the association is desperate to develop in the area and is convinced that there is a need to be fulfilled, both in new housing and also to create extra mobility.

The private house builder has concrete proposals for development and for the likely take up of private houses and flats. The planners se that a private development will be favored by the local people who have a negative view of "problem tenants".

There are therefore three parties to the negotiations that will ensue. The local authority, the private house builder and the housing association. The housing association has the hardest job of all, trying to persuade the local authority of the merits of allowing it to go ahead and develop and also trying to overturn the objections of the private house builder, even perhaps persuading them to enter into a joint partnership.

The strategy in this sort of negotiation, which is not a win-win situation but very much a situation which is stacked initially against the housing association, is for the association to have identified all of the variables, such as housing need, mobility options, and increased housing for those on lower income and also to have clearly identified its ultimate aims in the light of those variables.

A plan is needed, which involves changing the culture of the initial negotiations so that those in power, and those whose plan is favored are brought round to the way of thinking of the association. This will be achieved by clearly communicating the views of the association.

The private house builder will, initially probably be intransigent and will need to be persuaded of the associations case before considering possible proposals for a mixed development. However, in the first instance, profit will be the motive and the developers concern to maintain the status of the scheme so that potential buyers are not put off.

Both will be leveling their needs wants and desires towards the planners who hold power.

In order to gain something from the negotiations, the housing association has to clearly map out its strategy. All of the relevant variables have to be identified and prioritized. The association has to aim as high as possible but must be prepared to compromise, if the chance arises, and enter into a mixed development.

A lot rests on the attitudes of the planners and the private house builder. However, the association has the difficult job of persuading both parties that it should either be allowed to develop or to join forces with the private developer.

Clear communication of identified advantages, all advantages, is paramount. The association will gain nothing through the negotiations if the other side is not clear about the need or the advantages of participation. The need to be flexible is clear along with enhanced powers of persuasion.

Planning is the crucial element. This will give confidence and will enable the association to doggedly pursue its aims and not to crumble in the face of intransigence.

Exercise.

On the basis of the third case study outlined above put yourself in the place of the housing association and define your own aims and objectives putting together a strategy which will enable you to achieve your goal.

****

Glossary of terms

Communication: There is the process of everyday communication, which involves those we interact with on a regular basis, or there is communication in the field of business, which is where most, but by no means all, communication takes place

Concessions: Those aspects of any deal that must be arranged and agreed during the process of negotiation.

Empathy: The ability to put yourself in another persons place and to understand their point of view.

Negotiation is concerned with the relationship between two parties where the needs of both are largely in balance.

Objectives: Desired results. They need to be specific and measurable and linked to a timeframe.

Persuasion: Where you try, through subtle means, to bring the other parties round to your way of thinking.

Power: Factors, tangible or otherwise, that give one person an edge.

Stance: The position taken up by a negotiator at any particular stage or over any particular issue.

Strategy: A course of action designed to achieve specific objectives.

Trading: The process of arranging, and sometimes exchanging, concessions. This is an inherent element of the negotiation process.

Variables: The raw materials of trading. The elements of what you have and what you need.

Win-Win: A common way of referring to a satisfactory outcome for both parties.

****

Index

Acceptance, 20
Adolf Hitler 75
Aggressive, 37

Balance, 27
Bilateral negotiations, 55
Bridge building, 92

Closing, 23
Communication, 31, 32, 42, 44, 109
Confidence, 66, 90
Contractual situations, 82

Deception 76
Definition, 87
Dirty tricks 75

Emotion, 19, 42, 43
Empathy, 37, 88, 109
Escalating demands 78
Extreme demands 78

Influencing, 32

Legitimacy, 66

Magic, 19
Misrepresentation 76
Multilateral negotiations, 55

Neville Chamberlain 75
Non-verbal communication 77

Offer, 20, 21

Patience, 88
Personal attacks 77
Positional pressure tactics 78
Preparation, 19, 52, 55, 90
Projection, 36
Psychological warfare 76, 77

Reaching an Agreement, 82
Rejection, 20

Silence, 89
Specific variables, 65
Strategy, 20, 109

Tactics 75
Techniques, 19, 49

Variables, 51, 65, 110
Verbal communication 77

Win-Win, 22, 92, 110

****

All titles, listed below, in the Straightforward Guides Series can be purchased online, using credit card or other forms of payment by going to www.straightfowardco.co.uk A discount of 25% per title is offered with online purchases.

Law

A Straightforward Guide to:

Consumer Rights
Bankruptcy Insolvency and the Law
Employment Law
Private Tenants Rights
Family law
Small Claims in the County Court
Contract law
Intellectual Property and the law
Divorce and the law
Leaseholders Rights
The Process of Conveyancing
Knowing Your Rights and Using the Courts
Producing Your own Will
Housing Rights
The Bailiff the law and You
Probate and The Law
Company law
What to Expect When You Go to Court
Guide to Competition Law
Give me Your Money-Guide to Effective Debt Collection
Caring for a Disabled Child

General titles

Letting Property for Profit
Buying, Selling and Renting property
Buying a Home in England and France
Bookkeeping and Accounts for Small Business
Creative Writing
Freelance Writing
Writing Your own Life Story
Writing performance Poetry
Writing Romantic Fiction
Speech Writing
Teaching Your Child to Read and write
Teaching Your Child to Swim
Raising a Child-The Early Years
Creating a Successful Commercial Website
The Straightforward Business Plan
The Straightforward C.V.
Successful Public Speaking
Handling Bereavement
Play the Game-A Compendium of Rules
Individual and Personal Finance
Understanding Mental Illness
The Two Minute Message
Guide to Self Defence
Tiling for Beginners

Go to: www.straightforwardco.co.uk

NOTES-USE THE FOLLOWING PAGES TO MAKE NOTES AND OBSERVATIONS AS YOU EMBARK UPON THE PROCESS OF NEGOTIATION.

NOTES

NOTES

NOTES

NOTES

NOTES

NOTES

NOTES

NOTES

NOTES